PRESENTED TO

BY

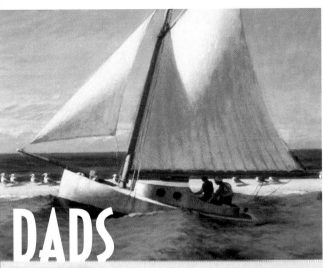

DADS

WALKING FAITHFUL, STANDING STRONG

Steve Farrar

COUNTRYMAN

Published by J. Countryman, a division of Thomas Nelson, Inc, Nashville,
Tennessee 37214.

Project editor—Terri Gibbs

Unless otherwise indicated, all Scripture quotations in this book are from the New
American Standard Bible (NASB) © 1960, 1962, 1963, 1971, 1972, 1973, 1975, and 1977
by the Lockman Foundation, and are used by permission.

Published in consultation with the literary agency of Alive Communications,
1465 Kelly Johnson Blvd., Suite 320, Colorado Springs, CO 80920

Designed by Koechel Peterson & Associates, Minneapolis, Minnesota

ISBN: 0-8499-5672-2

www.jcountryman.com

Printed and bound in the United States of America

CONTENTS

ACTIONS

*T*here are two ways that fathers teach. First, they teach with their lips. Every father uses his lips to instruct his children about right and wrong. The second way that a father teaches is with his life.

Corrie Ten Boom, in her book, *In My Father's House*, once recounted a lesson her father taught her with his life. At the time, Corrie was a young woman working with her father as an apprentice watchmaker in Holland. Their house was attached to their shop and every morning after breakfast she would make her way through the door of the kitchen into the shop to begin work.

The words a father speaks to his children in the privacy of his home
are not overheard at the time, but, as in whispering galleries, they will be
clearly heard at the end and by posterity.

—RICHTER

actions

It was a time of financial hardship for the family. In fact, they had a large bill that was many months overdue. Corrie had been praying for weeks with her father that God would provide the money to pay off the bill.

One morning a very wealthy man from the community entered the shop. He asked Corrie's father to show him several of the most expensive watches in the store. There was one in particular that caught his eye. Corrie was silently praying that God would prompt the man to buy the watch so they could pay their debt.

The man put the watch down on the counter and pulled out a large roll of bills. She could not believe that anyone would carry that much cash. He counted off the bills to Corrie's father and she was silently thanking God for His provision. Her prayers had been answered!

As her father was putting the money into the register, the gentlemen asked her father, "Did you know Mr. Van Houten? He was my watchmaker for years."

"Yes, I knew him," replied Mr. Ten Boom. "He was a fine craftsman. His death has been a real loss to his family. But his son has taken over for his father."

"Yes, I realize that. I actually bought a very fine timepiece from his son, but it wouldn't keep time. I took it to him three times for repair and he could never get it right."

"Do you have it with you?" asked Ten Boom.

"Yes," said the man and he pulled it out of his pocket.

Mr. Ten Boom took the watch and opened up the case. He made a small adjustment and then said to the gentlemen, "I think that will fix the problem. It was just a small mistake. It should work just fine for you now. Sir, I know that young man, and he is a fine watchmaker. I believe that he is just as good as his father. I think it would encourage him if you would buy your new watch from him instead of me."

The man was shocked at the suggestion of Corrie's father. And so was Corrie!

"Sir, this young man has had a very difficult time without his father. But he will learn. If you have a problem with any of his watches, just bring them to me and I will make sure the problem is corrected. Please allow me to give you back your money. I think it would be best if you bought the watch from the young man."

The startled man took his money and made his way out the door.

Corrie looked at her father and then glanced at the nearly empty cash register, which had been full just a moment before.

"How could you do such a thing?" she asked her father.

"Corrie, you know that I brought the gospel at the burial of Mr. Van Houten."

Corrie writes:

> Of course I remembered. It was Father's job to speak at the burials of the watchmakers in Haarlem. He was greatly loved by his colleagues and was also a

very good speaker; he always used the occasion to talk about the Lord Jesus.

Father often said that people are touched by eternity when they have seen someone dying. That is an opportunity we should use to tell about Him who is willing to give eternal life.

"Corrie, what do you think that young man would have said when he heard that one of his good customers had gone to Mr. Ten Boom? Do you think the name of the Lord would be honored? There is blessed money and there is cursed money. Trust the Lord. He owns the cattle on a thousand hills and He will take care of us."

Corrie had a father whose God wasn't money. His God was Jesus Christ. He taught his daughter a lesson that morning that stayed with her for the next sixty years. He taught her not only by his words but by his actions.

Train up a child in the way he should go, and when he is old, he will *not depart from it.*

—PROVERBS 22:6

Confidence is courage at ease.

— DANIEL MAHER

A FATHER'S

*P*aul Getty Jr. rarely saw his father. When your father is the wealthiest man in the world, it is not unusual for him to be all over the globe doing business. Paul Jr. was not close to his father, although he wanted to be. His visits were few and far between. Like any young boy, he wanted to sense the approval, acceptance, and affirmation of his father.

When he was in high school, he wrote a letter to his father. The letter came back from his father, with all of the spelling errors marked and the grammatical mistakes underlined in red. There was no personal note. All his father did was take the time to point out the boy's

"*This is my beloved Son* in whom I am well pleased."

—MATTHEW 3:17

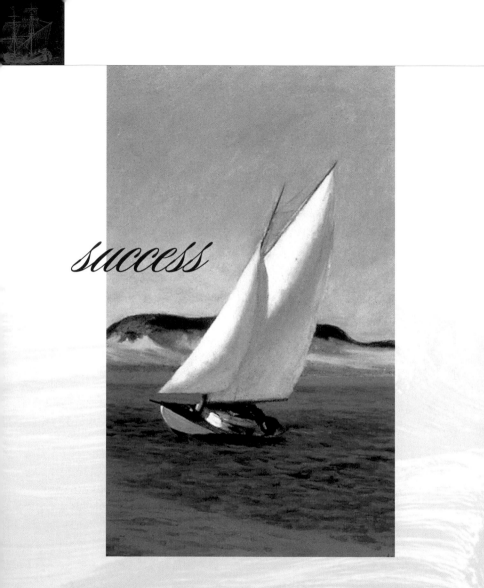

success

mistakes. In the words of Paul Getty, Jr., "I never got over that."

The singer Marvin Gaye was about to sign a huge record contract with Motown Records in 1978. But then Marvin made a demand that stopped everything in its tracks. He stated that he wanted a million-dollar signing bonus. And he wanted it handed to him in cash in a briefcase. The record company refused. When they asked Marvin why he wanted a million in cash, he replied, "I want a million dollars cash so I can take it to my father and say, 'See this? That's a million dollars. I just want you to know how successful I am.'"

Marvin Gaye was seeking the approval of his father.

Dads never stand taller than when they give affirmation and appreciation to their children.

Sons and daughters need to hear their father's approval. In the same way that God the Father expressed from heaven His verbal appreciation for His Son, so we earthly fathers need to follow His example.

So what are some practical ways to express approval to our children?

1. Express your approval with your words.

So often what is in our hearts never gets communicated from our lips. I talked with a man this weekend who is forty-eight years old. He told me that his father is still living and he appreciates and deeply loves his father. He knows his father loves him. But never once in his life has he heard his father say, "Son, I love you."

I asked him about his relationship with his own children. "I tell them verbally that I love them all the time," he said. "I want them to *know* how special they are to me."

God the Father loves us with an everlasting love. And He expresses that love to us all the time through the pages of the Bible. That love is an unconditional love. He loves us in spite of our sins and shortcomings. When we are disobedient, He loves us by disciplining us. But we can never do anything that will keep Him from loving us.

2. Express your approval about character, not just accomplishments.

As dads we get excited when our kids bring home straight A's or hit the game-winning home run. And we should get excited. But what should really turn our cranks is when our kids take steps in character development. Now that's something to get excited about!

When your son comes to you and admits he didn't tell you the truth, what do you do? Do you jump on him? I don't think so. When we come to the Father and admit our sin, does He jump on us? No. He accepts us and forgives us. So we should do the same with our children. When a child comes and admits a lie or deception, he should receive grace, and should be commended for his honesty, in spite of the earlier deception or lie.

When your daughter eats lunch at school with the girl who is not popular, commend her! Get a bass drum and start a parade. That's a character issue and your daughter should be praised to high heaven. She did the right thing and it was hard. So commend her for that act of kindness.

You've heard of the Good Housekeeping Seal of Approval. You've undoubtedly got it stamped on some appliances around your house. Make sure your kids know that they have your Good Heart-Keeping Seal of Approval.

I will speak ill of no man, and speak all the good I know of everybody.

—BENJAMIN FRANKLIN

RESPECT

*W*hen I was a sophomore in high school, I walked out of the locker room after a football game one night. Two of my friends pulled up and said, "Steve, we've got a case of beer in the back seat and we're heading to a party at the beach." What really got my attention was not my two friends, but the three girls in the car with them. One of them, I was particularly interested in. And when she said, "Come on, Steve, there's room for you to sit with me," I was *definitely* interested.

Then I remembered that my dad had just told me on the field to be home by eleven o'clock,

"*My father was frightened of his father, I was frightened of my father, and I am going to see to it that my children are frightened of me.*"

—KING GEORGE V

since I had to get up early and go to work in the morning.

I seriously considered getting in that car, but I knew I would never get back from the beach by eleven. So I declined the invitation and said I had to go home.

I really wanted to go.

But I really *didn't* want to face my dad when I came in after curfew.

I was tempted, but I decided it just wasn't worth what it would cost. If I came in late, I'd have to face my dad. If I told him the truth, I'd be in big trouble. And if I lied, and he found out later that I lied, I'd be in even bigger trouble! My dad loved me and he didn't mess around. He made sure we knew that disobedience was not worth while.

And I'm sure, the fear of facing my dad kept me out of a lot of trouble that night.

There are two kinds of fear: healthy fear and paralyzing fear.

Moses, in addressing the fathers of Israel, refers to the right kind of fear:

> *Now this is the commandment, the statutes and the judgments which the Lord your God has commanded me to teach you, that you might do them in the land where you are going over to possess it, so that you and your son and your grandson might fear the Lord your God, to keep all His statutes and His commandments, which I command you, all the days of your life, and that your days may be prolonged.* —DEUTERONOMY 6:1-2

How does a child learn the fear of the Lord? I believe he learns about the fear of the Lord by first learning the fear of his father. Not the kind of fear that King George was referring to, however. I don't mean that a child should walk around terrified of his father. Absolutely not!

We are not to live in terror that God might strike us down at any moment, are we? Of course not. Neither should a child live in that kind of fear of his father. So, what does this mean?

respect

The healthy fear of a father is simply that the child knows the father means what he says. When the father sets a rule, it is to be obeyed. If it is disobeyed, the child will receive appropriate consequences. The purpose of all of this is not to abuse a child, but to *train* a child.

If a father doesn't teach his children that he means what he says, why should they believe God means what He says?

We have so many families in America without any leadership and direction. I call these families "drifting families." They drift along, governed by a cultural current that can take them into many dangerous places. A father who loves his family does not allow it to drift along the river of life. He sets parameters for his children. He sets rules that are for their benefit.

God does the same for His children.

The fear of the Lord is a healthy and awesome respect for God and His word. Yes, He loves us with an unconditional love. And because His love is so great He will discipline us when we wander foolishly away from His commands. He loves us too much to let us get our own way.

In the book of Proverbs, the fear of the Lord is mentioned fourteen times. And in every case, we learn something valuable about what the fear of the Lord does for us.

• PROVERBS 1:7: The fear of the LORD is the beginning of knowledge; fools despise wisdom and instruction.

• PROVERBS 1:29: Because they hated knowledge and did not choose the fear of the LORD.

• PROVERBS 2:5: Then you will discern the fear of the LORD and discover the knowledge of God.

• PROVERBS 8:13: The fear of the LORD is to hate evil; pride and arrogance and the evil way, and the perverted mouth, I hate.

• PROVERBS 9:10: The fear of the LORD is the beginning of wisdom and the knowledge of the Holy One is understanding.

- PROVERBS 10:27: The fear of the LORD prolongs life, but the years of the wicked will be shortened.

- PROVERBS 14:26: In the fear of the LORD there is strong confidence, and his children will have refuge.

- PROVERBS 14:27: The fear of the LORD is a fountain of life, that one may avoid the snares of death.

- PROVERBS 15:16: Better is a little with the fear of the LORD, than great treasure and turmoil with it.

- PROVERBS 15:33: The fear of the LORD is the instruction for wisdom, and before honor comes humility.

- PROVERBS 16:6: By the fear of the LORD one keeps away from evil.

- PROVERBS 19:23: The fear of the LORD leads to life, so that one may sleep satisfied, untouched by evil.

- PROVERBS 22:4: The reward of humility and the fear of the LORD are riches, honor and life.

• PROVERBS 23:17: Do not let your heart envy sinners, but live in the fear of the LORD always.

Do you know what I find so interesting about Proverbs? When you read the opening verses, you find it's a book in which a father is teaching his son how to live life wisely. And isn't it interesting that this father does exactly what Deuteronomy six said he should do: He is instructing his son in the fear of the Lord.

A few years ago, one of my sons was telling me about his friend who had gotten into big trouble. As we discussed the boy's problems, my son, who was then fourteen, said, "You know what the real problem is, Dad?"

"No," I replied. "What is it?"

"When you get right down to it, he has no fear of his father. He knows that his dad doesn't mean what he says. His dad has never followed through and disciplined him. That's the real reason he's in trouble."

Quite frankly, I was stunned at my son's analysis. Just the

night before he had been upset when I wouldn't let him stay out later than his curfew.

But in his heart he knew what his friend's real problem was. His friend had no fear of his father.

Healthy fear can keep a kid out of trouble.

It sure worked for me thirty-five years ago.

And I'm doing my best to pass the tradition on to my kids.

Spend your life

for something

that will outlast it.

—WILLIAM JAMES

A DAD'S PRAYER:

THERE'S NO LAW AGAINST IT

*P*rayer used to be part of the basic fabric of American life. And there are still a few remnants left in our culture. The Senate begins each session with prayer. But recently, a Hindu priest was invited to give the prayer in the Congress of the United States. Did the Founding Fathers ever in their wildest dreams imagine something like that?

For generations, school children began their day with prayer. High school football games would never kick off without a local minister opening in prayer, asking God to protect the boys and enable them to be good sports.

Those days are quickly fading into the past.

Someone recently handed me a prayer that was written by a high school student in Arizona. I don't have the original source, but I think it's worth duplicating here as fodder for thought.

THE NEW SCHOOL PRAYER

Now I sit me down in school,
where praying is against the rule,
for this great nation under God,
finds mention of Him very odd.

If Scripture now the class recites,
it violates the Bill of Rights,
and any time my head I bow,
well that's a federal matter now.

Our hair can be purple, orange, or green,
that's no problem, it's a freedom scene.
The law is specific, the law is precise,
prayers out loud are a serious vice.

You stand tall when you kneel to pray.

—AUTHOR UNKNOWN

For praying in public might offend someone,
and that is something that just can't be done.
In silence alone we must meditate,
for God's name must be separate from the state.

We're allowed to cuss and dress like freaks,
and pierce our noses, ears, and cheeks.
Hate speech is outlawed, but first the Bible,
to speak of a verse will make me liable,

We can elect a pregnant senior queen
and the unwed daddy our senior king,
but it's not allowed to teach right from wrong,
we're taught that "judging" does not belong.

We get our condoms and birth controls,
then study in class witchcraft and totem poles.
But the Ten Commandments are not allowed,
no sure word of God must reach this crowd.

It's scary here I must confess;
when lawlessness reigns, the school's a mess.

So, Lord, this silent plea I make…
should I be shot, my soul please take.

This is a disturbing poem, but it drips with reality.

I have a friend who is a very good father. He takes very seriously his responsibilities as a father of five children. His daughter is a freshman in a school not too far from my home. Last week, a fifteen-year old kid pulled a gun and took his teacher and classmates hostage. I heard about it over the radio. That night, as I watched the national news, there was no mention of the incident. Five years ago, that story would have led off the news, but now it's almost a weekly occurrence.

When it comes to school prayer, may I make a suggestion. The schools are finished praying. That's pretty clear. But there is no law that keeps a father from praying for his children while they are in school.

There is no law that keeps you from taking a moment in the morning to pray with your kids before they leave for school.

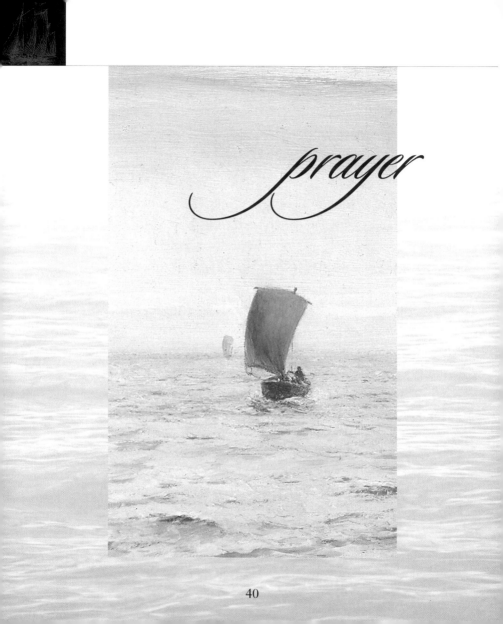

prayer

There is no law that keeps you from breathing prayers for them throughout the day while they are in school.

There is no law that keeps you from praying at the dinner table when they get home from school.

When it comes to prayer, the real issue is not what is the school doing. The issue is what is Dad doing.

HOW MUCH

DO YOUR KIDS NEED?

Leo Tolstoy used to tell a story about a rich nobleman and the peasant who lived on his land. One day the rich landowner told the poor man that he appreciated all of his hard work over the years. In appreciation, he would give to the peasant all of the land that the man could walk around from sunup to sundown. Whatever ground he could cover would be his.

The next day the peasant started walking at sunrise. His walk was more like a jog. He was trying to pace himself, for he had the whole day ahead, but he wanted to make the most of this once-in-a-lifetime opportunity. He pushed

There are two ways to get enough. One is to accumulate more and more. The other is to desire less.

—G. K. CHESTERON

riches

himself all morning, and then reluctantly, at the urging of his wife, agreed to sit for a few moments to eat some soup and rest. But after a few minutes he quickly got up and resumed his race for the land. By mid-afternoon, his lungs were burning and there was a pain in his side, but he kept pushing.

Mercifully, the sun finally set and the light was gone. The man had physically given everything in order to get his land. Exhausted, he walked into his house, sat down at the table for dinner, and died of a heart attack.

The next day, his friends lowered his body into a plot of ground that was six feet deep, seven feet long, and four feet wide.

And then Tolstoy asked the question, "How much land does a man really need?"

I have three children. Only one of them is still at home. The years have absolutely flown by. And in just three more years, we'll have an empty nest.

In looking back over my years as a father raising children, I made a mistake. In fact, I have made many mistakes. One of the mistakes that I made was that I gave my kids too much.

My kids have too much and may I say that your kids probably have too much. It's something we fathers tend to do. And we're encouraged in this by our culture.

When my daughter, Rachel, was two, we threw a birthday party for her. Now it was my understanding that birthdays worked a certain way. You sent out invitations to your friends and invited them to your party. There was ice cream and cake for everyone. Friends came with gifts. Everyone played games and had a wonderful time. That was how you did a birthday party.

But things had changed in thirty years.

We invited all the kids in the neighborhood over for Rachel's party. There was ice cream and cake galore. Everyone brought a present for Rachel. Then when it was time for the children to leave my wife gave each child a present. That part was new to me.

I asked Mary about that after the party, and she told me that was the new custom. Instead of the birthday kid getting presents, every kid at the party gets a present. (Sounds like a government program to me.)

Frankly, I think that's a mistake. It's one thing to honor a kid because it's his birthday. It's another to give every kid a gift at the party so he won't feel left out. We didn't used to do that. But now we're prosperous. Too prosperous. And we're spoiling our children.

Last night, my three young nephews came by to show us their awards from YMCA soccer. Each of them came in holding a nice trophy. Then they showed me a gold medal around each of their necks.

When I was a kid, our team got a trophy. The rest of us got a hot dog. Now kids each get a trophy plus a gold medal the size of Rhode Island.

Is this not a little much?

Yes, I've given my kids too much over the years. I've made that mistake from time to time. Thankfully, they're all three very hard workers. I'm grateful to God for that. I didn't damage them completely.

To those of you who currently have children at home, may I give you a tip: Your kids don't need *things*, they need *you!*

It's great to give them appropriate gifts at the right time. Every good father delights in doing that. But the greatest gift you can give them is *you*.

After all, that's what they really want.

They want you.

Time with you.

If you're going to give them too much of a good thing, why not give them that?

We make a living by what we get, but we make a life by what we give.

—NORMAN MacEWAN

SETTING
LIMITS

ood fathers set limits for their children. But they also have to set limits for themselves.

In the next three chapters, we're going to look at one of the greatest threats to being a good father. Actually, there are two threats but they're closely intertwined.

The first is *career*.

The second is *money*.

Both of those issues can quickly become silent viruses that affect our decisions and behavior as dads.

Where there is most labor there is not always most life.

—HAVELOCK ELLIS

A number of years ago, I read a remarkable article in *Fortune Magazine* about a man named Dennis Levine. In the article, Levine was as honest and forthright about his struggle with career and money as anyone I've ever read. He was a good family man, but he got ambushed. And he shared his story because he didn't want other husbands and fathers to fall into the same trap. By his own admission, Dennis Levine was exceptionally ambitious, exceptionally successful, and exceptionally affluent—and it ruined his life.

Dennis Levine made history when the disclosure of his misdeeds exposed those of Ivan Boesky, his illicit partner, who, in turn, led the government to Michael Milken and Drexel Burnham Lambert. After the legal skirmishes ended, Levine had to spend time in jail. But it really didn't add up. He came from a good home, had a loving wife, with one child and another on the way. What was he doing in jail? Coming from a middle-class background, he had made it without any help. He had worked hard, took classes in the evening, and eventually earned an MBA. What was this guy doing at Lewisburg Federal

Prison in Pennsylvania?

Levine tells it in his own words. And he does it with the hope that his experience will be a warning to others. That's why he now lectures in colleges and universities. He tries to warn students of the inherent dangers to a life lived without limits. Success, ambition, and money nearly destroyed his life.

Levine writes:

"Why would somebody who's making over $1 million a year start trading on inside information? That's the wrong question.... When I started trading on non-public information in 1978, I wasn't making a million. I was a twenty-year-old trainee at Citibank with a $19,000 annual salary. I was wet behind the ears, impatient, burning with ambition.... Eventually, insider trading became an addiction for me. It was just so easy. In seven years, I built $39,750 (gathered from family loans and credit card cash advances) into $11.5 million, and all it took was a twenty second phone call to my offshore bank a couple of times a

limits

month…. My account was growing at 125 percent a year compounded.

And Wall Street was crazy in those days. These were the 1980s, remember, the decade of excess, greed, and materialism. I became a go-go guy, consumed by the high-pressure, ultra competitive world of investment banking. I was helping my clients make tens and even hundreds of millions of dollars…. The daily exposure to such deals, the pursuit of larger and larger transactions, and the numbing effect of sixty to one hundred-hour work weeks eroded my values and distorted my judgment.

At the root of my compulsive trading was an inability to set limits. Perhaps it's worth noting that my legitimate success stemmed from the same root. My ambition was so strong it went beyond rationality, and I gradually lost sight of what constitutes ethical behavior. At each new level of success I set higher goals, imprisoning myself in a cycle from which I saw no escape. When I became a senior vice president, I wanted to be a managing director, and when I became a managing director, I wanted to be a client. If I was making $100,000 a year, I thought, I can make $200,000. And if I made $1 million, I can make $3 million. And so it went. Competitive jealousy is normal in business. Everybody wants to make more than the guy down the hall. By the time I made partner at Drexel, I was out of control…. We all regularly put in time on weekends and after 7 or 8 P.M., when the partners usually knocked off for the evening. The hours were so obscene that my family ribbed me about being a wage slave. But I loved my work. I realized, Hey, I'm doing this, and I'm doing it well."

In light of Mr. Levine's candid account, let's look at a statement made by the wisest and once the richest man in all of history, King Solomon: "Do not weary yourself to gain wealth" (PROV. 23:4). That flies in the face of most American men.

I'm not saying there's anything wrong with having riches if God allows them to come your way. It is wrong, however, to expend all of your energy in the quest for more and more. Some economic systems prohibit people from improving their lot in life. That is wrong as well. Different economic systems operate on diverse principles.

Levine admits that his motives were not noble. Pure and simple, he wanted to get rich. So he wearied himself to gain riches. He had to work unbelievable hours during the week and then work some more on the weekends. He portrayed these hours as "numbing"—numbing hours that eroded his values and distorted his judgment. To his credit, he now tells other businessmen about the importance of spending time with their families. He wearied himself to gain riches, and found that it was not worth the effort. By the way, how is your schedule these days?

Have you built in any limits?

If not, why not?

You will find as you look back upon

Your life that the moments

when you have really lived

are the moments when you have done

things in the spirit of love.

—HENRY DRUMMOND

MORE

*D*ennis Levine found out that making
$100,000 a year wasn't enough. Neither was
$300,000 or $1 million or $3 million. How
much are you currently making? How much
do you think it would take to give you a sense
of satisfaction? Levine discovered that no
matter how much he made, it didn't bring
satisfaction. He found out firsthand what
Solomon discovered thousand of years ago:
Money cannot bring satisfaction. But there's
another warning about money to be found in
the New Testament.

"Those who want to get rich fall into temptation and a snare and many foolish and harmful

He who loves money will not be satisfied with money.

—ECCLESIATES 5:10

desires which plunge men into ruin and destruction" (1 TIM. 6:9). Earlier in this same passage, the Apostle Paul said in essence that men who do not provide for their families are worse than pagans (1 TIM. 5:8). As fathers, God has given us the responsibility to provide for our families. But we have to set limits on this task. If we don't, it can kill us.

Do you want to *Think and Grow Rich* as the popular book title promises? Then be very careful. C. H. Spurgeon put it this way: "It is a very serious thing to grow rich. Of all the temptations to which God's children are exposed, it is the worst, because it is the one they do not dread. Therefore, it is the more subtle temptation."

Wanting to get rich is a subtle temptation. A subtle temptation to sin. And the reason it is subtle is that we think it can't hurt us. The fact of the matter is it can destroy us.

In Levine's transparent account, he describes how the pursuit of more and more money was a snare. His desires became foolish and harmful. And he was plunged into ruin and destruction. According to Levine, "Saying good-bye to your family is painful enough, but try explaining to a five-year-old why Daddy is going to prison."

Dennis Levine is not the first man to discover that the desire to be rich can plunge men into ruin and destruction. In his book, *Waking from the American Dream*, Donald McCullough shares this information.

"In 1923, seven men who had made it to the top of the pyramid met together at the Edgewater Hotel in Chicago. Collectively, they controlled more wealth than the entire United States Treasury, and for years the media had held them up as examples of success.

Who were they? Charles Schwab, president of the world's largest independent steel company; Arthur Cutten, the greatest wheat speculator of his day; Richard Whitney, president of the New York Stock Exchange; Albert Fall, a member of the President's Cabinet; Jesse Livermore, the greatest bear on Wall Street; Leon Fraser, president of the International

money

Bank of Settlement; Ivar Kruegger, head of the world's largest monopoly. What happened to them? Schwab and Cutten both died broke; Whitney spent years of his life in Sing Sing penitentiary; Fall also spent years in prison but was released so he could die at home; and the others—Livermore, Fraser, and Kruegger—committed suicide."

Paul was right. Those who want to get rich don't realize they are flirting with ruin and destruction. And there's another thing they usually don't think about: the uncertainty of riches. We hear so much today about "financial security." There's nothing wrong with financial planning. But there's everything wrong with thinking that your financial planning will bring you security for the future. Security for your future rests in Jesus Christ. Period.

What are the chances that you or I will ever have the financial portfolio of Schwab or Cutten? "The chances are slim and none," as they say in Texas, "and Slim just left town." Do you think that Schwab and Cutten had any idea when they walked into the Edgewater Hotel in 1923 that they would die broke? I seriously doubt it. If anyone has any doubt that riches are uncertain, a brief look at the "financial security" of Schwab and Cutten should erase it.

Keep your life free from the love of money. Be content with what you have. For God has said, "I will never desert you nor will I ever forsake you." Hence we can confidently say, "The LORD is my Helper, I will not be afraid; what will man do to me?" (HEB. 13:5–6)

Stacey Woods knew all about financial security. But he didn't learn it on Wall Street. He learned it from his parents. His parents had a ministry of establishing churches in the outback of Australia. In his biography, *Some Ways of God,* this founder of the Intervarsity Christian Fellowship in America, tells of the faith of his father, which taught him much about the security of trusting in God.

> Father had a profound trust in God and His promises. He took Matthew 6:33 literally (But seek first His kingdom and His righteousness;

and all these things shall be added to you). God had promised to meet his need. He never had a salary, never took up an offering for his ministry nor authorized anyone else to do so, never asked anyone for personal support.

This quiet confidence on the part of both my parents—for Mother stood one hundred per cent with Father—made a deep impression on me. Trusting God for everything was part of our life....

Once in his caravan days Father and his fellow worker had finished up every crumb of food for breakfast. And neither of them had a cent to buy more. It came time for the midday meal. To the astonishment of the younger man, Father said, "Let us lay the table for dinner."

"But we have no food," exclaimed his companion.

"God has promised that we shall not go hungry. We must honor him by our faith in His promise."

The table was set, glasses filled with water.

"Let us sit down and give thanks for our meal," said my father. Heads were bowed and thanks returned.

As the prayer ended, a knock sounded on the caravan door. There stood a woman they had never seen before. "Me and my man are having a chicken dinner and thought you fellers might like some." She had walked more than a quarter of a mile across the fields bringing that chicken dinner with all the "fixins."

Woods then makes this comment to those of us in contemporary society. "The trend of government is to undergird us with material securities from the cradle to the grave, providing all kinds of insurance—health, old-age, education, unemployment and so on. In addition, we insure ourselves against fire, earthquake, hurricane, and accident. These safeguards are not wrong, but they can easily become a serious hindrance to our complete trust in God. Undoubtedly, if our debts are paid and our refrigerator full, if we have money in the bank, we have the tendency to feel secure in ourselves, and our need of God is less. Herein lies the danger. My greatest need is to feel and know my need of God every hour."

As a Christian father, have you ever asked God to protect you from the lure of getting rich?

It's a wise prayer to pray. And every time you do, you're setting wise limits.

AGUR'S
LIMITS

*I*n 1893, Richard D. Armour was worth fifty million dollars. That's a lot of money today. It was much more back then. He had built his meat packing business from the ground up until he had fifteen thousand employees. In spite of his enormous wealth, Armour got up at five each morning and drove to the plant. There he stayed, this mighty transformer of meat into money, until six in the evening, at which time he went home for dinner, followed by a nine o'clock bedtime. "I have no other interest in my life but my business," he told an interviewer. "I do not love the money. What I do love is the getting of it."

With the catching ends the pleasure of the chase.

—ABRAHAM LINCOLN

What Armour loved was not only the reward but the chase.

We serve what we love. Armour loved making money more than money itself. But he still had to serve somebody.

- When you love the reward more than Christ, you've got a problem.

- When you love the chase more than Christ, you've got a problem.

- And when you love your career and the pursuit of wealth, more than your family, you've got another problem.

John Piper provides some needed perspective in his book, *Desiring God:*

> "Picture 269 people entering eternity in a plane crash in the Sea of Japan. Before the crash there is a noted politician, a millionaire corporate executive, a playboy and his playmate, a missionary kid on the way back from visiting grandparents.

After the crash they stand before God utterly stripped of Mastercards, checkbooks, credit lines, image clothes, how-to-succeed books, and Hilton reservations. Here are the politician, the executive, the playboy, and the missionary kid, all on level ground with nothing, absolutely nothing in their hands, possessing only what they brought in their hearts. How absurd and tragic the lovers of money will seem on that day."

In the movie "Wall Street," there was an insightful comment: "The problem with money is that it makes you do things you don't want to do." That's what bad masters do. They enslave their followers. That's the pity of choosing to serve money.

Are you familiar with a man in the Bible named Agur? He prayed one of the most unusual prayers in the Bible. And it concerned money. The prayer to which I refer is recorded in Proverbs 30:7–8:

> *Two things I asked of You,*
> *Do not refuse me before I die:*
> *Keep deception and lies far from me,*

rewards

Give me neither poverty nor riches.

Agur asked God to bless him by granting him two requests. The first request was that God would enable him to be a man of truth. He asked God to keep deception and lies far from Him. That was a very wise prayer.

The next request is the unusual one. What is unusual is that Agur asked God *not* to give him two things. First of all, He asked God not to give him poverty. We would all say amen to that request. But then, in the same breath, he asked God *not* to give him riches. You won't hear too many folks say "amen" to that one.

Why in the world would Agur ask God not to give him riches? I appreciate David Roper's perspective on this in his book *The Strength of a Man:*

> Early Christians would have abhorred our pursuit of ease and affluence. Back then no one would have believed that becoming a Christian could place a man among the rich and famous. Today for some it's

considered a divine right. Some say that sickness, poverty, and infamy are signs of unbelief and that God wants us all to be healthy, wealthy, and wise. Apparently then, the only victory that demonstrates closeness to God is full healing and circumstantial happiness. If only it were so.

Such a theology of success simply isn't so; God saves greater things for us than mere earthly happiness. Unscriptural and unrealistic expectations can plunge us into despair and unbelief and cause us to ignore what's really taking place."

Agur in essence was saying, "Dear God, please, I ask of you, whatever you do, don't give me riches." We have no quarrel with Agur when he asks God to keep him from deception and poverty. But most of us would choke on the request to not have riches. In this day and age, to not want riches is almost non-Christian.

Why in the world would Agur make such a request? The answer is simple. He was setting limits. On the one hand, he asked God not give him poverty. That was one limit. On the other, he asked God not to give him riches. That was another. Agur wanted to stay within wise limits. He didn't want poverty, he didn't want riches, he just wanted enough to make his mortgage and car payment, put some away for retirement, and get his kids through college.

As I read it, Agur was asking God to keep him in the middle. He was the original cheerleader for the middle class. When was the last time you heard anyone express a desire to be middle-class? Agur was asking for middle-class because he was setting some limits.

Are you staying within your spiritual limits when it comes to money or have you been going over your limits? What are you pursuing? Are you pursuing Christ or riches? Are you interested in the ultimate financial portfolio? If you are, then here is the prospectus for genuine financial security: Seek *first* the kingdom of God, and all of these things will be added unto you.

In your heart of hearts, what are you seeking?

Remember this, that very little is needed to make a happy life.

—MARCUS AURLIUES

NINE TRAITS

William Beausay, in his excellent book, *Boys!*, cites the good wisdom of Vance Packard. Packard spent a lot of time thinking about parenting, and especially fathering. He suggested nine skills that would make fathers and mothers more effective with their children.

1. Skillful child-developers make it clear that they are crazy about that particular child.

Do your children know that about you? Do they know that you're crazy about them? Do they understand that you think they are the best? Last night, I overheard by wife talking to my daughter on the phone. Rachel is a senior

It's harder to lead a family than to rule a nation.

—CHINESE PROVERB

in college in California. She's been going through some discouragement over the last few weeks and is burned-out academically and emotionally.

I heard Mary saying to her, "Rachel, do you know we love you? Do you know how gifted and special you are? Do you know how proud we are of you? What you're going through is part of the ebb and flow of life, but don't let it keep you from forgetting how much we love you. We're on your team!"

Kids need to know their parents think they're number one, whether they're twenty-one years old or twenty-one days old.

2. *Skillful child-developers do much interacting, especially verbal, with the child.*

Computers, video games, television, and portable CD players with headphones are enemies of fathers who want to talk meaningfully with their children. But those things can also be escapes for fathers and give them an excuse not to talk with their kids.

All of those things have their place. But they cannot be allowed to intrude into the family. It's hard to compete with CD's, video games, and the Internet. Parents didn't have that kind of competition fifty years ago. But we sure have it now. Talking with our kids has always been a challenge. It's even more so today.

3. *Skillful child-developers work to help the child develop a high level of self-esteem.*

I hesitate to mention this one and the reason is this: our schools and culture have taken an emphasis on self-esteem to ridiculous heights. I'm sure you've heard it, too. "Giving a child a failing grade will hurt his self-esteem." "Disciplining a child will hurt his self-esteem." This kind of thinking damages children.

But there is a legitimate self-esteem that we must work to instill in our children. If a child knows he is loved, if a child is disciplined, if a child is protected, if a child is made to do his chores, he will have the right kind of self-esteem, and not the synthetic type offered by the liberal experts of our day.

lead

4. Skillful child-developers condition children to do well.

Too often we reward our children when they don't achieve or discipline themselves. That's a mistake. They should know they are loved regardless of their achievement, but they should be encouraged to do their best. There are verbal rewards and physical rewards. When you give your best effort, don't you appreciate being rewarded, even is some small way? So go and do likewise with your children.

5. Wise child-developers encourage children to be explorers.

Did someone encourage you to read when you were a boy? That's exploring! Maybe a shop teacher let you try things at his workbench after school. That's exploring. Exploring is not just what Columbus and Magellan did. Exploring is a channeled curiosity that needs to be encouraged in the lives of our children.

6. Good fathers try to give their children a sense of family.

I believe it was Pat Conroy who said that every family is a small civilization. Children need to know that the world doesn't revolve around them. And a good place to discover this is within the family unit. Everyone in the family has different gifts, talents, personalities, and strengths. But we are stronger together than we are apart. So we work through our conflicts instead of letting them divide us. We help each other, we pray for each other, we encourage each other, and we stick together. Just like another family called the church.

7. *Skillful child-builders are good at moving children from parental discipline to self-discipline.*

The job of fathering is to help each child grow to become a responsible adult. This means there has to be a major transition that moves a child from doing something because you told him to, to doing something because he knows he should. Without self-discipline there will be no success, accomplishment, or well-being in your son or daughter's life. That's the destination!

8. *Skillful fathers guide their children to a set of values.*

This should really be number one on the list. And where

do these values come from? They come from God and His Word, the Bible. Deuteronomy 6 makes it very clear that fathers are to teach their children the truth of God's Word. Morality comes from His moral law. His law is absolute. His law is fixed; it cannot be changed. That's where morality and law come from. It's your job to teach your children that truth is absolute and not relative.

9. *Expert child-raisers help their children experience plenty of responsibility.*

"He who is faithful in a very little thing is faithful also in much" (LUKE 16:10). Responsibility is the name of the game in life. Maturity is synonymous with responsibility. So we start to teach this concept early with our children. Pets must be fed and cages must be cleaned. Clothes must be picked up and toys put away. Dishes must be cleared from the table and taken to the sink.

You know the drill.

It's what you do every day.

PERFECTIONISM

*D*r. H. C. Morrison had a tremendous ministry
before he went home to be with the Lord.
He founded a school that influenced thousands
of young men for Christ. Morrison tells the
remarkable story of how he was influenced
for Christ.

As a young teenage boy, Morrison was working in the fields of his father's farm. He was
not a Christian. As he was working, an old
Methodist circuit-riding preacher rode by.
Over the years, he had watched this man ride
his appointed rounds to preach the gospel. He
knew of the man's reputation and character.
The young man paused from his work to

Could everything be done twice everything would be done better.

—GERMAN PROVERB

watch the old preacher ride off into the distance. Suddenly, Morrison felt the power of God's presence, and right in the middle of the field, the conviction of God came over him. He immediately dropped to his knees and gave his life to Christ.

Not a word was exchanged between the old man and the young man. But the Spirit of God used the example of a holy man to bring conviction to young Morrison.

Holiness is not a popular topic for discussion anymore. But a father can't give anything more important to his children than the example of a holy life.

And what does it mean to be holy? Does it mean that a man must quit his job and become a preacher? Of course not. Holiness begins with simply being in the presence of God.

This is exactly what happened to Isaiah:

> *In the year of King Uzziah's death I saw the Lord sitting on a throne, lofty and exalted, with the train*

of His robe filling the temple.

Seraphim stood above Him, each having six wings: with two he covered his face, and with two he covered his feet, and with two he flew.

*And one called out to another and said, "Holy, holy, holy, is the **Lord** of hosts, the whole earth is full of His glory."*

And the foundations of the thresholds trembled at the voice of him who called out, while the temple was filling with smoke.

*Then I said, "Woe is me, for I am ruined! Because I am of unclean lips, and I live among a people of unclean lips; for my eyes have seen the King, the **Lord** of hosts"* (ISA. 6:1–5).

What is holiness? Holiness is moral purity. God is the essence of holiness. It is His primary trait. And when Isaiah was in the presence of the Holy One of Israel, he immediately became aware of his own sin.

May I make a very practical application right here? Have you ever been around someone who was super-spiritual? By that

I mean that person wore his goodness and perfection on his sleeves. Super spiritual people make others feel that they're slightly beneath them. That's a false spirituality.

The first step to personal holiness is to realize not that you are above people but that you are the chief of sinners! When you get a glimpse of the holiness of God, the last thing you're going to do is make someone else feel they're one step below you.

Men of holiness are easy to be around. They're down-to-earth. They're not trying to impress anybody. They're all too aware of their own sins and shortcomings. The old country preacher was not putting on airs with anyone. He didn't have a holier-than-thou attitude. He knew he was a great sinner who had received a greater mercy.

Some fathers tend to be perfectionists. They make life difficult for their children. Their kids feel that no matter what they do, they can never measure up to the high standards of Dad.

Cheap grace is grace without discipleship.

—DIETRICH BONHOEFFER

grace

The cure for perfectionism is a glimpse of the holiness of God. When you realize the moral perfection of God, it permanently puts to rest your meager attempts to demand so much from others. A glimpse of the holiness of God takes the rough edges off of perfectionist fathers. The holiness of God has a way of putting you on your face in gratitude for His mercy and grace and kindness. And that in turn causes you to be kind to others.

Young H. D. Morrison was not converted by the preacher's sermon. He was converted by a sweet humility in the man's spirit. Just watching that humble and unassuming man ride his horse gave him a glimpse, not of the greatness of the preacher, but of the greatness of his God.

I don't know about you, but as a dad, I could use a good dose of that sweetener myself.

God is honored by honesty

and steadfast endurance

rather than by escape from duty.

—PHILLIP VOLLMER

ELEPHANTS

AND RHINOS

I was looking through the television channels one night not long ago and hit on a gold mine. It was one of those animal shows on public television. And the lesson stopped me dead in my tracks.

One of the huge game preserves in Africa had a problem. The elephant population had grown too large and, as a result, was overgrazing the land and foliage. Park officials decided that a good solution would be to move part of the herd to another game preserve.

Now it's one thing to move a herd of cattle, but it's another to move scores of elephants.

One father is worth more than a hundred schoolmasters.

—GEORGE HERBERT

Officials determined that the best way to pull off this mammoth undertaking was by helicopter. They designed a special sling and, one by one, the elephants were transported to their new home. But a problem quickly surfaced.

The female elephants and their young offspring were easily transported. But when the sling was put around a fully developed male elephant, the helicopter couldn't lift the gargantuan animal off the ground. It's weight exceeded the weight capacity of the helicopter. After numerous attempts at solving the problem, the officials decided not to transport the males. Only the females and young elephants were moved.

The transition seemed to be progressing just fine. But gradually another problem developed at the game preserve. For some unexplainable reason, white rhinos began turning up dead. White rhinos are relatively rare and are favorite targets of poachers, but poachers always take the horns of the rhinos. And that was the first tip that poachers weren't involved—each of the dead rhinos had its horn. It had not been removed.

This was a great mystery. Who was killing the white rhinos? To solve this mystery, the rangers turned to technology. They set up cameras around the park. It wasn't long until the culprits were caught on tape. The rangers were shocked to discover they had a gang problem on their hands. Some young adolescents had gotten together and decided it would be fun to kill white rhinos.

Their strategy was very simple. They singled out a rhino and chased it until it was exhausted. Then, when the rhino could run no more, they closed in as a group and killed the exhausted beast.

Yet the officials were still puzzled. Why were these adolescents acting like this? It was discovered that they were running wild because they had no mature, male supervision—which is always the case with a gang. Gangs are almost always comprised of boys who do not have fathers to supervise and discipline them. And here again, that point was proven. But in this case, the culprits weren't young boys. The gang members killing the rhinos were elephants!

No one had ever seen such behavior among elephants. Rangers throughout Africa were stunned. But it didn't take long for an explanation to surface. These young elephants had no male supervision. They were part of the group that had been transferred from another game preserve along with their mothers... *without* the male elephants.

To resolve the problem the park rangers arranged to bring in some older male elephants. In less than a month, they observed an astonishing behavior change among the rogue adolescent males. They didn't travel in packs anymore. They spent time in the presence of the elder males. And the elder males were making it very clear that the unruly behavior was not acceptable.

The problem was solved. What the young male elephants needed was male oversight!

That's also true of the young males in your home and your community. They need strong male leadership.

That's why God gave us fathers.

Fathers draw lines. They reward appropriate behavior. They discipline when the lines are crossed.

That's what keeps young males (and females, I might add) from getting into trouble.

It's the formula for keeping society safe and sane.

If you don't believe that, just ask the white rhinos.

OBEDIENCE

Lloyd Ogilvie tells the story of a teenage girl who spent several weeks at youth camp. While she was there, she was challenged to submit all of her life to the Lordship of Christ. She decided to commit everything in her life to the Lord—her future, her hopes of marriage and a family, her desires and dreams. She didn't want to be a halfway Christian. She wanted to love God with all of her heart, soul, mind, and strength. It was her desire to serve the Lord completely as she returned home to begin another year of high school.

When she arrived at home, her father asked, "How was camp?"

The godly take God seriously.

—CHARLES R. SWINDOLL

committed

"It was great, Dad!" she replied. "I decided to commit every area of my life to Christ. I want to yield to Him in everything. I want Him to run my life!"

And then she turned to her dad and asked, "Dad, have you ever done that?"

The father was shocked that his daughter would ask such a direct and private question. He was somewhat angry and flustered, but he tried to hide it. He brushed off her question with some trifling comment, but he couldn't get it out of his mind.

Not only was he a member of a church, he was on the Board of Trustees. He had taught Sunday school for years. But there were other things in his life. His business was extremely important to him. He had scratched and clawed to build it up over the years, and he held it in very tight control. Over the years he had also accumulated a substantial financial portfolio. And he wasn't about to give up control of that to anyone. Not even God.

He prayed for his children and their well being, but he never sought God for guidance in his business decisions. He was a self-made man. Of course, he believed in Christ, but he didn't want to take things too far.

As the weeks and months went by, he observed changes in his daughter's attitude and behavior. No longer was she just going through the motions of attending church. She was intent about it now. She actually seemed to have a personal relationship with Christ. He was real to her. And if the truth were known, Christ was not very real to him.

Eventually, the example of his daughter's life forced him to admit that he was a religious man who desperately needed Christ. With great humility and shame, he bowed his head and asked God to forgive him. He gave himself completely to the Lord. He surrendered control of his whole life, including his business and his financial holdings. And he asked forgiveness for not leading his family spiritually the way he should have.

This man was not the first to be led to repentance by a

young girl. In the Bible, we read about Naaman, who was a great general in the army of the king of Aram (2 KINGS 5). But this highly respected general and brave warrior had leprosy. There was a young Jewish girl working in his household, who told Naaman's wife about the God of Israel and his prophet, Elisha. In turn, his wife told Naaman and the general searched about the country to find the prophet. When he arrived, Elisha sent him a message instructing him to go and dip in the Jordan River seven times. Naaman was greatly offended. The Jordan River was a mere stream compared to the rivers in his homeland. Who did this prophet think he was, telling an army general to dip in a common river? He was outraged. But after he calmed down a bit, some of his men reasoned with him. Eventually, he decided his response had been unreasonable, and with humility of spirit, he went back to the Jordan and dipped seven times as Elisha had instructed him.

His willingness to obey indicated that he was submitting to the Lordship of the God of Israel. He had to lay aside his pride and his posturing about his own status, and humble himself before God.

That is what living a godly life always comes down to: obedience. Obedience to the One who created you. Obedience to the One who gave you your gifts and position... obedience to God.

He is Lord. He owns everything. We don't. And He can take it away in a minute to remind us that we are not in charge.

One day every knee will bow, and every tongue will confess that Jesus is Lord. It is the wise father who bows before Christ now. And sometimes God will use our own kids to teach us that lesson.

Strong faith and living hope are the best result of unconditional commitment to Jesus Christ.

—BILLY GRAHAM

THE ESSAY

*M*ost of this book has been written on an Apple computer in my home office in Dallas. But I'm writing these words at a Carl's Jr. hamburger stand in Pismo Beach, California. We have all gathered out here at my mom and dad's house. It's Thanksgiving weekend, and we've had a great time. It has also been a difficult time. This is the first Thanksgiving we've ever spent without my brother, Mike. Last May, he suffered a massive coronary as he walked into his office early one morning. We've all been trying to adjust to life without him. When our family would get together, Mike was the one who arranged most of the

112

Live your life in such a manner that when you die the world cries and you rejoice.

—OLD INDIAN SAYING

fun. We had a great dinner Thursday afternoon but Mike wasn't there.

Friday morning the boys all went fishing, and that night we all went down to the beach and grilled the fish. After dinner we turned the coals into a roaring bonfire and sang songs and roasted marshmallows. It was a great time, but Mike wasn't there.

Mom and dad were there, I was there with my family, and Mike's family was there. But Mike wasn't. I've been pondering that the whole weekend. In fact, in the middle of Thanksgiving dinner, I had to fight back tears when I looked up and saw Mike's picture on the wall looking down on us.

I came over to the hamburger joint this morning to do some writing. As I was looking on the hard drive for my work, I noticed a file entitled "Mike Farrar." Now remember, this is my mom's laptop I'm using. When I saw that file I decided to open it. And what I found was an essay about Mike written a couple of years ago by his son, Jason.

Jason is now thirteen, so he was eleven when he wrote this.

Mike Farrar

Mike Farrar still wishes he had a full head of hair but, hey, life is not always fair. Maybe he has not lost much hair, but I always make fun of him because of it. He is a tall person, and rather big in the mid-section. He wears a black suite every day to work except on Friday, Saturday, and Sunday. In his spare time or when he's at home he wears shorts and a collared shirt.

He loves to play sports. Football is his favorite sport. He always watches football whenever there is a game on. He got a scholarship to USC (University of Southern California). Then he injured his knee so he couldn't play anymore. Golf is another of my dad's favorite sports. It isn't his best sport, but I think it lets him relax. He also likes to wrestle. He enjoys going to my meets and watching me pin the other person.

When it comes to doing something wrong, there's my

life

dad. No matter what, he is always on top of things. Sometimes it's good but sometimes it's bad. My dad loves his job. He'll take me to work with him sometimes and let me file for him, but most of the time he doesn't take me. He is a straight-up Christian. In other words, he does it all for God. He goes to church every Sunday and teaches a Bible study for my church.

My dad is a really funny guy. He makes jokes that are so funny. Like I said earlier he likes to wrestle, and sometimes he'll wrestle with me for fun. Maybe my dad looks a little scary but inside he's a big softy.

This is a small book about fathering. I was going to write something else this morning. But when I came across this short essay by Jason I knew I had to include it.

In a sense, Jason's essay became a eulogy.

My brother was forty-eight years old when he died.

Most of us guys think we're going to be around at least seventy maybe eighty years. But we never know for sure do we?

Moses put it well in Psalm 90:10–12:

As for the days of our life,
they contain seventy years,
or if due to strength, eighty years,
yet their pride is but labor and sorrow;
for soon it is gone and we fly away...
So teach us to number our days,
that we may present to You a heart of wisdom.

You may have forty years left or you may have four days. Nobody knows. Mike didn't know last Thanksgiving that he wouldn't be with us this Thanksgiving. You don't know that you'll be around next Thanksgiving.

So what does that mean?

It means that we need to ask God to teach us to number our days so that we might have a heart of wisdom before Him. Wisdom to live biblically, wisdom to make the right choices, wisdom to be the best fathers we can possibly be.

Life on earth isn't forever. This Thanksgiving, Jason didn't have his dad. He only had memories of his dad. Are you living wisely today? That's important to consider because one day your kids are going to remember. They may even write an essay.

L'AMERIQUE SEPTENTRIONALE

Suivant les
Nouvelles Observations
de
Messrs de l'Academie Royale
des Sciences, etc.
Augmentées de Nouveau.

A AMSTERDAM
Chez COVENS et MORTIER

Lieues d'Allemagne de 15 au Degré
Lieues de France de 20 au Degré

TERRES

D. de Jaq. Lancastre

Baye d'Hudson

Assenipoils

CANADA ou NOU
L. Superieur

Lac des Tintons

fort Bon Secours

Quivira habité par les Aïahos

Pays des Illinois

Apaches de navaio fort etendus vers l'Ouest

Apaches Yaguero

Apaches de Xila

Coama ou Cosmana

MEXIQUE

NOUVEAU

FLORIDE

Sonora

Cinaloa

Californie

Nouv. Biscaye

los Zacatecas

Panuco

GOLFE DE MEXIQUE

Cuba

Nouv. Albion

R. Brave